The
Mentoring
Revolution

About
Daniel Cohen

Daniel Cohen is the Founder and CEO of Graduway, the leading provider of alumni networking and mentoring platforms with clients across 58 countries.

Daniel is recognized as a leading thinker, writer and speaker in Career Services and Alumni Relations. In 2015, he was named as one of LinkedIn's Top 10 Influencers in Education.

He is the author of many articles and books including 'The Alumni Revolution' and 'Alumni Therapy'.

Daniel also chairs the Graduway Leaders Summit, a multi-yearly gathering of leading global executives to discuss best practice and strategic trends in student mentoring, career opportunities and alumni engagement.

Graduway®
Empowering
Alumni Relations

Table
of
Contents

1	**CHAPTER ONE** THE CASE FOR MENTORING

12   The Case for Mentoring

14   Do Engaged Alumni Really Give More?

18   Bursting the Higher Education Bubble with Alumni Career Services

20   Making the Case for Funding Career Services & Alumni Relations

2 CHAPTER TWO
THE FUTURE OF MENTORING

25 The Future of Mentoring

26 5 Big Mentoring Mistakes

28 Why Can't You Scale Your Mentoring?

30 Must Alumni Mentoring Relationships Be Like 'Marriages'?

32 Should Alumni Mentoring Be A Dating App or An Arranged Marriage?

35 The Tech Revolution in Alumni Networks

37 The Anatomy of the Ideal Mentoring Program

3 CHAPTER THREE
MENTORING BEST PRACTICES

40 How to Yield 42% Participation in an Alumni Mentoring Program?

43 The Value of Engaging Your Young Alumni

44 What is Stopping You from Fulfilling Your Potential?

46 Say Goodbye to Your Graduating Class. Forever.

48 Are You Crazy? Don't Build It Yourself. Buy.

50 The Benefits of Speed Mentoring

52 7 Top Tips to Improve Your Mentoring

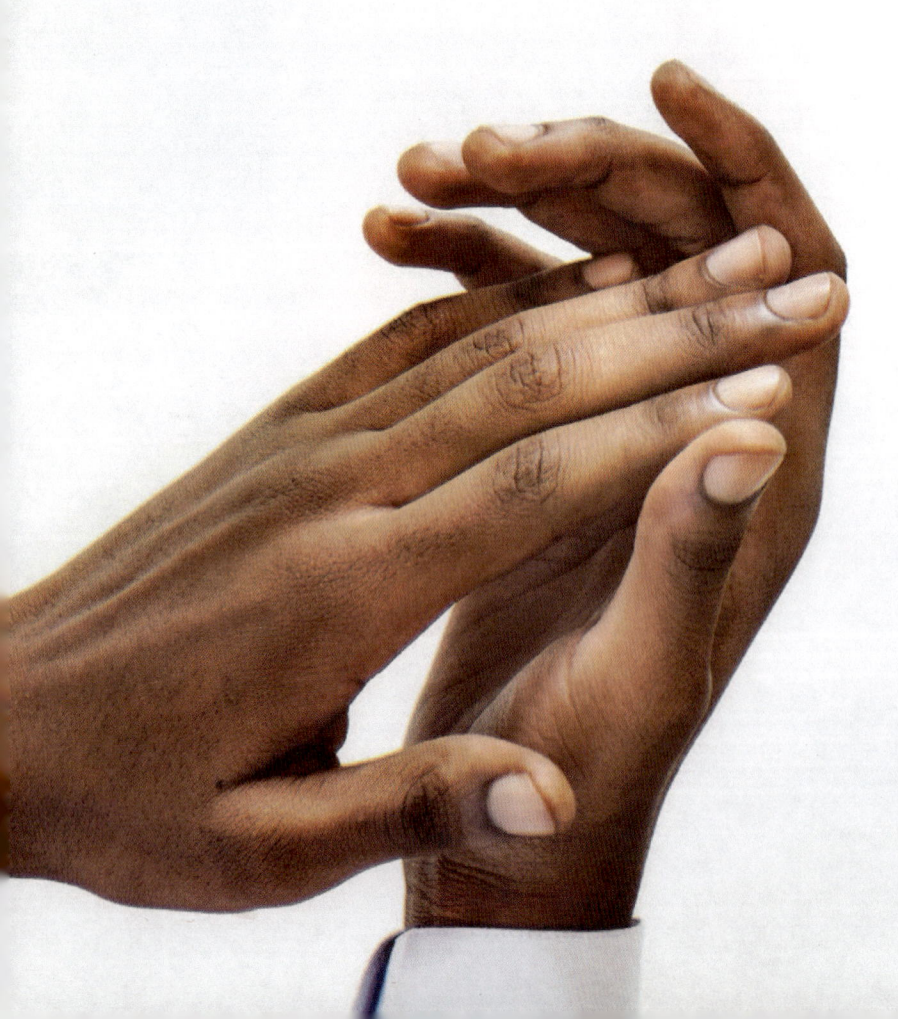

Introduction

The Age of Mentoring Has Arrived.

Gone are the days when mentoring was the luxury of just the few. Today, mentoring has become the necessity of the many.

The demand for mentoring is on the rise.

Students and Alumni - they all want and expect to have access to mentors. Also, they each have a different definition of what that mentoring looks like – be it professional or social, intense or light touch.

Today, many schools are looking at their mentoring programs as a key way to rediscover their unique value proposition; to alumni on the one hand, and to prospective students and parents on the other.

For alumni – one of the strongest ways to drive engagement is by asking alumni to give back as a mentor while also having the opportunity themselves to access a willing network of mentors. Engaged alumni disproportionately give back their time, talent and treasure to their alma mater.

For students (and parents) - there is no better way to show the unique value of your school than by providing access to a mentoring network. The focus on employability and life-outcomes strikes at the core concerns of parents when selecting which school, college or university to send their children.

The challenge is how do schools transform their small existing mentoring programs, which typically cater for hundreds of students and alumni, into programs that can meet the needs of thousands?

In short, how do schools make mentoring available for the many and not just the few?

I entitled this special report 'The Mentoring Revolution'.

For some, the word 'Revolution' may seem like hyperbole - an exaggeration. I beg to disagree.

There is a 'Revolution' taking place both in the demand and supply of mentoring.

On the demand side, I will contend that parents and governments alike are relentlessly looking at our education institutions and evaluating their true impact. Career and life outcomes from studying at schools will become a dominant measure of success, a strong indicator of the return on investment from education. Moreover, it seems that one of the biggest interventions a school can make to improving those career and life outcomes is through its mentoring programs.

On the supply side, schools are understanding that they are ill-equipped both culturally and technologically to meet this growing demand. Simply increasing the number of people working career services will not be sufficient to meet this overwhelming demand. The solution will have to involve leveraging digital technology to meet such large numbers and, almost as importantly, a shift in culture to think about mentoring as a necessity for the many, not the few.

'The Mentoring Revolution' seeks to understand this challenge and suggests practical steps to scaling mentoring programs by leveraging digital; seek in effect to mentor those responsible for mentoring programs.

The opportunity is clear. Every school can transform their mentoring into scalable, global, flexible and ultimately hugely value-adding programs.

It is also worth noting that this 'Revolution' applies to all education institutions: from K-12 schools all the way to Higher Education. This book is aimed at those responsible for mentoring irrespective of country, type or size of institution.

This special report is built upon a combination of my individual essays, both new and old, which are bite-sized to allow the reader to easily dip in and out of this special report. These essays have been consolidated around three key themes.

The first chapter deals with The Case for Mentoring and expounds the value in building deeper student, parent and alumni relationships by facilitating vibrant mentoring programs. This chapter seeks to provide the arguments on why schools must invest more in mentoring. The return from mentoring programs will be reflected firstly with improved student enrolment and secondly higher alumni giving.

The second chapter explores The Future of Mentoring. What will mentoring need to look like in say 10 years from now? This chapter explores the cultural and technical barriers to achieving this vision and the obvious mistakes to avoid. It is about understanding what is preventing us from scaling our mentoring.

The third chapter is a practical guide to Mentoring Best Practices. This chapter shares some examples of best practices which I have seen. Included in this is who owns the mentoring relationship within each school - career services, alumni relations, both or neither? What is needed to ensure your mentoring programs will be successful in the long-term?

Throughout this special report I make numerous recommendations of videos to watch which can be found on **Graduway's Youtube Channel**.

I owe a huge debt of thanks to the hundreds of career services and alumni relations professionals with whom I have spoken.

My daily conversations with you have enabled me to clarify my own thoughts about the challenges and opportunities facing our profession.

I would like to call out the contributions of Chris Marshall and Sheila Curran, both in advice and in allowing me to interview them for a number of essays. They are incredible thought leaders in their respective areas, Chris starting his journey from the alumni relations perspective and Sheila from the career services perspective. This special report is intended in some way to be the mid-point of where these two views meet.

'The Mentoring Revolution' doesn't provide all the answers, nor is that its purpose. Rather, this book seeks to ask key questions which I hope will inspire your institution to initiating those tough internal conversations and making the necessary interventions that are right for you.

The Revolution is coming.

Mentoring for the many and not the few.

Daniel Cohen
March 25, 2018

- CHAPTER ONE -

The Case for Mentoring

The Case for Mentoring

The provision of mentors to students and alumni used to be a low priority for education institutions.

A service offered by the career services department to the few.

Simply put, it was a 'nice to have'.

Not anymore.

Mentoring is fast being recognized as perhaps one of the most, if not the most, critical components of our formal education experience, and key in driving the long-term success for college alumni.

At a CAAE Institute Winter Meeting in Scottsdale Arizona, I had the privilege of hearing a remarkable presentation by Brandon Busteed, the Executive Director Education and Workforce Development for Gallup, of a study commissioned with Purdue University. Brandon outlined what drives long-term alumni success and the role alumni organizations can have in impacting graduates' well-being.

For anyone working in a University, I don't think it gets more fundamental than improving the long-term well-being, both socially and financially, of their graduates.
The Gallup-Purdue study found that where you went to college matters less to your work life and well-being after graduation than how you went to college.

The study found that students being 'emotionally supported' during college improved the chances of them being engaged in their work more than two-fold, and the chances of thriving in their well-being more than three-fold. Moreover, one of the most important ways to be emotionally supported is by having 'had a mentor who encouraged their goals and dreams'.

Just 22% of respondents could answer affirmatively that they had access to such a mentor. As Brandon put it,

"Feeling supported and having deep learning experiences during college means everything when it comes to long-term outcomes after college. Unfortunately, not many graduates receive a key element of that support while in college: having a mentor. And this is perhaps the biggest blown opportunity in the history of higher ed."

Imagine that you were a school providing mentoring programs to most students and not just these lucky 22%.

Imagine if your school could statistically demonstrate the provision of mentors to virtually all students and hence forecast these life and career outcomes decades from now.

What competitive advantage would this give your school when speaking with prospective students and parents?

These outcome statistics would rightly dominate your school's marketing and enrollment strategies.

Now think more negatively. What if you did NOT provide mentoring but your closest rival school did? What would be the impact on your enrollment?

If providing mentors to the many is such a clear benefit to schools, why not provide mentors to most of their students and alumni?

Firstly, there has been a general lack of awareness of the importance of student alumni mentoring.

Secondly, schools tend to think about facilitating mentoring in very resource heavy and unscalable ways. The careers department often will manually match and connect individuals to each other. This takes up a lot of time and is obviously not suitable if you need to do this for thousands of students.

The answer lies in a combination of leveraging your alumni and technology.

Your alumni are a readily available army of experienced and motivated mentors willing to help and guide your students. In fact, you probably only need around 5-10% of your alumni to volunteer to have more mentors than you need.

Technology has also changed, meaning that you can literally provide alumni software or an alumni directory within days and enable students and alumni within the alumni portal to choose and connect with each other.

The onus will clearly remain on students to take advantage of the mentoring opportunities being made available to them. However, let's at least provide that opportunity to our students.

Moreover, I believe there is an argument that facilitating mentoring should be a life-long service offered to students and alumni alike.

The case for mentoring seems clear. How will schools respond to this opportunity?

Do you agree with the case for schools to provide mentors?

Do you have experience of implementing such a provision and what were your biggest challenges?

I look forward to exploring this with you.

Do Engaged Alumni Really Give More?

When making the case for mentoring, we normally focus on the career/life outcomes of students.

However, the other side of this same coin is the benefit of building deeper relationships with mentors who are disproportionately alumni.

Have you ever wondered whether there is a correlation between the level of alumni engagement and donor participation rates?

If you ask most education institutions, they will probably answer yes, there is a correlation, that mentors and volunteers make their best donors.

However, beyond that, it appears difficult to state the exact correlation and the direction of any causation.

Are engaged alumni more likely to become donors or are donors simply more likely to be engaged alumni?

A case study of Tulane University's on-line mentoring and alumni network provides us with more insights on this correlation. (Disclaimer - their career network is powered using software from my company Graduway.)

Christine Hoffman, Senior Associate VP for Individual Giving at Tulane University, said that regarding the 10,000 alumni using their on-line career and mentoring network, "Over 50% of our alums using the platform are donors.

That is a significantly higher number than our overall donor participation rate."

Over 50% is an astonishing figure. Especially when there are a very large number of alumni using the platform.

Often, we are asked to make a 'return-on-investment' argument on why an education institution should invest in a mentoring or career network. This used to be an incredibly difficult thing to do until now.

Tulane University's example is to show the massive value of every school investing in their alumni relationships irrespective of the direction of the causation between mentoring engagement and financial giving.

In a worst-case scenario, they have invested in building a career community that is disproportionately valuable to their donors. 5,000+ of their donors are using the platform.

In a best-case scenario, they are directly contributing through their alumni engagement to deepening and widening their relationships.

The old question of *can we afford to invest in mentoring* is being replaced with a new question *can we afford not to?*

I would welcome your thoughts.

Bursting the Higher Education Bubble with Student and Alumni Career Services

I attended the ASU GSV Summit in San Diego and heard an interesting keynote from Dan Rosenzweig, CEO of Chegg.

Dan's presentation discusses not if there is a bubble in higher education but whether it is about to burst?

Dan eloquently explains all the data and analysis which, I agree, seems to point to a bubble and to the fact that we are probably close to the 'bursting point'.

The bubble appears to be due to an in-balance in the value equation for Higher Education. The high and increasing price for college is simply too high for the current value proposition being offered. Falling demand from students combined with over-supply from education institutions points to a bubble.

Where I have a different line of thinking is not if there is a bubble in Higher Education or whether it is about to burst but, maybe more importantly, what options exist for colleges to 'manage' this bubble.

There are three broad strategies that I think could be adopted:

1. Do Nothing

Let market economics work their magic and deal with the over-supply by some/many institutions eventually closing their doors.
If you believe that the 'bubble' is not evenly distributed and will affect other institutions more than your own then this could make sense. This might make sense particularly for Ivy League+ schools.

2. Restructure

Another option is a combination of reducing prices for college education combined with cost cutting to make institutions more competitive. In short, this is increasing demand by providing a cheaper and possibly a lower quality product to students.

3. Improve Value Proposition

This final option involves looking at the underlying value equation being offered to prospective students and finding new ways to justify that premium price.

If I were a Dean or Chancellor, I would focus on the third option and I would invest in two areas that I think can improve the value equation relatively quickly and significantly.

Firstly, I would invest significantly more in career services including alumni and student mentoring. A Gallup/Purdue University study last year pointed to the importance of receiving a mentor while a student in achieving improved life-time outcomes. Moreover, I believe the more a college can do to demonstrate how they provide superior career services, the stronger the premium they can justify. Parents, in particular, will appreciate this value when quantifying the return on investment from a college education.

Secondly, I believe investing more in alumni career services. Your alumni are your institution's most important asset and building relationships with them is the equivalent of the business world investing more in their corporate marketing. Alumni are your brand ambassadors. The greater the alumni network, the greater the premium to your institution that can be justified. This also complements improved career services as your alumni will be an integral part of your students' career community.

Although I believe there is a bubble in Higher Education, I also believe this can be managed properly through increasing the value equation offered to students via career and alumni relations services.

Do you agree that there is a bubble in Higher Education?

If yes, which strategy do you believe is the best way to manage this bubble?

Finally, do you agree that investing in career services and alumni relations is the best way to re-balance the value equation for students?

Making the Case for Funding Career Services & Alumni Relations

The education world is under pressure.

Public funding is falling. Tuition fees are rising. Cost cutting is everywhere.

Yet, I hear consistently from schools on how they are under-resourced in terms of both headcount and budget. In fact, some would go as far as to claim that their's is the most under-resourced department.

In such a tough macro environment, making the case for increasing funding is a challenge.

Speak to your Dean or Vice-Chancellor about increasing funding and you may get a standard response that surely there are other more pressing and urgent areas for investment.

We seem unable to articulate clearly enough that Career Services & Alumni Relations are an urgent priority and not a 'nice to have'.

I think there are two main reasons why we are failing:

1. Short-term thinking

Education institutions need results quickly from investments they make. Building your brand through your ambassadors is critical to the long-term health of the school.

2. Measuring the wrong things

The key performance indicators for leaders in education are usually student numbers, research or teachings scores and not long-term alumni career and life outcomes.

So, what can be done?

Instead, one measure your Leadership will surely listen to concerns ranking.

The good news is that the major external rankings are increasingly putting greater emphasis on alumni feedback and their outcomes.

For example, Bloomberg Businessweek requires 30% of a graduating class to respond to its survey to qualify to enter their rankings. The Financial Times alumni responses contribute a staggering 59% of their ranking's weight.

So, in short, when you are making that proposal to increase... yes, talk about the long-term health of the school, and yes, talk about enrollment and development.

But, let's be smarter. Let's talk about the short-term impact on rankings as well as the long-term brand building that will come from investing more.

I would welcome your thoughts.

CHAPTER TWO

The Future of Mentoring

The Future of Mentoring

What will mentoring look like in the future? Let me share 8 possible predictions:

1. For the Many and not the Few

The first and most obvious observation is that mentoring will cease to be a small and exclusive subset of a student body. Mentoring for the masses is an irresistible trend for those institutions that want to stay relevant.

2. Student-Alum vs. Alum-Alum Mentoring

Second is the expansion of mentoring from a purely student-alum pasttime to becoming a core part of the wider alumni network. The future will be that one person can be both a mentor and a mentee! Mentoring is for life and schools needs to support this.

3. Technology Enabled

No longer will matching be manually done. Career Services will facilitate large scale mentoring by leveraging mentoring and alumni networking software.

4. Social as well as Professional

The definition of mentoring will broaden from the primary focus today of a strong professional bias to a much broader definition. Lifetime outcomes for students are not just career based but are much broader than that, including the full breadth of social interactions.

5. Facilitated rather than Controlled

Mentoring relationships will be less controlled by the central Career Services department. Their role will shift from micro-managing to enabling and facilitating mentoring. There may well be less control over the mentoring, but its overall impact will be greater.

6. Heavy vs. Light Mentoring

Mentoring relationships will no longer have to be this deep, long-term, heavy commitment and will be much more flexible, lighter and more spontaneous. Yes, there will still be a place for long-term, deep mentoring relationships, but these will be the minority. Flash mentoring is the future!

7. Mentoring as a Critical KPI

Mentoring will cease to be a 'nice to have' and will become a core metric that the leadership of every education institution tracks and seeks to improve.

8. Mentoring Ownership

The mentoring relationship will cease to be owned by either the Career Services or Alumni Relations department but will be owned by one department which will be established to cover both.

Do you agree with my vision of the future of mentoring?

I would welcome your thoughts.

5 Big Mentoring Mistakes

If, like me, you are convinced that all our students need a mentor, what is the best way to make this happen?

The answer lies in using a combination of both technology (alumni network and mentoring software) and a large group of capable and willing mentors (your army of alumni).

However, too often, I see well-intentioned schools making 5 big mentoring mistakes. They are as follows:

1. Not providing a scalable solution

Manually pairing off students with alumni, one at a time, is not a scalable solution and requires too many resources and man-hours. The goal here is providing all students with the opportunity to have a mentor. To do this, you must provide alumni software where students and alumni can pair themselves off with each other, by the thousands, and without the direct intervention of the school. The school's role here is simply one of facilitation.

2. Not providing sufficient value for mentors

Usually it is much harder to get mentors (alumni) rather than mentees (students) to join the platform. What is the value proposition to, and the motivation for, mentors joining your platform? As such, to have successful alumni mentoring or student mentoring program, you cannot have it as a stand-alone module. It will only work if it is part of a wider alumni networking platform where there are reasons for your mentors to be engaged and active such as

jobs, events, photos, discussions, etc. A strong alumni networking platform will lead to a strong mentoring platform within it.

3. Micro-managing users

There is a fine balance between facilitating mentoring relationships and micro-managing those relationships. Having connected with each other via your platform, your mentors and mentees are quite capable to organize when, how and where they will communicate going forward. Features such as appointment scheduling, in my opinion, look both clumsy and interfering.

4. Not making the mentoring specific enough

Providing willing alumni is a good start. However, the mentees need to know specifically what each mentor is willing and unwilling to do. Mentoring means something different to each of us. The more specific and granular you can make each mentor's willingness to help, the more likely the mentoring introductions will be successful.

5. Not making mentoring relevant for your community

The type of mentoring offered needs to be specific and relevant to your community. For many, this is purely about professional mentoring by finding a mentor in your chosen industry or profession. However, for others, it can be social and even spiritual - students finding life coaches and role models that can provide valuable support through their shared gender, sexuality, ethnicity, nationality, etc.

Mentoring is a critical offering for all education institutions.

I hope my highlighting these 5 big mentoring mistakes can improve our chances of doing it right whether you work with students, alumni or alumni career services.

Why Can't You Scale Your Mentoring?

Ask a typical school to rate how strong is their mentoring program.

The typical answer goes something like this:

"We have a world-class mentoring program.

We have been working on it for years and are righty proud of our achievements.

Each mentee has individual attention from us. We can find the perfect match for them.

We are also able to track and monitor every step of the mentoring relationship.

We know when they meet, how often and for how long they meet.

We get amazing survey results from mentees and mentors alike.

And our repeat mentoring statistics are incredible.

In fact, our mentoring program is outstanding in every way possible except one metric."

What is that 'one metric'?

"The number of people in a mentoring relationship is tiny."

In fact, as a percentage of the total student population, the number of mentoring relationships is embarrassingly small. Typically, well under 5% of students are in a mentoring relationship.

Education institutions are rightly proud of the quality of mentoring but when asked to aggressively expand the quantity of mentoring relationships, they find a much harder challenge. Short of hiring more people, how do you scale your mentoring?

Virtually every school, college and university are grappling with the same issue.

How do you get both quality and quantity when it comes to mentoring?

I believe there are two major barriers to achieving a mentoring program that can truly scale:

1. Technical Barriers

It is not humanly possible to continue to manually match mentees and mentors other than for the smallest, most exclusive programs.

Leveraging digital technology is the only way to bring mentoring to the masses so that you can scale.

2. Cultural Barriers

While well intentioned, the expectation that each and every step of the mentoring relationship should be controlled and montored is not feasible. The reality is that insisting that every step of the mentoring interactions take place on your digital platform is simply too restrictive for most mentors.

In short, scaling your mentoring program will come at two costs.

The first cost is the actual cost of acquiring the right digital mentoring technology. This is still far cheaper than increasing headcount, but is still a significant cost.

The second cost is on control and quality. To achieve mentoring for the many, you will need to compromise on the level of control that you have over the mentoring relationships. This allows for mentoring that fits into the lives of your mentors and mentees, and not necessarily the approach that gives you the best data. This means allowing mentoring to take place outside of the narrow constraints of your mentoring platform.

Your role is to facilitate mentoring for the many and not to stifle it. For example, you can keep control and quality through surveys and other feedback tools.

The price of scaling your mentoring is a price worth paying to bring mentoring to the many and not the few.

I would welcome your thoughts.

Must Alumni Mentoring Relationships Be Like 'Marriages'?

A question for both alumni relations and career services professionals – must alumni mentoring really be like marriage? I don't believe so.

Let me explain.

For a while now, I have seen two somewhat contradictory statistics.

On the one hand we have seen 70% of alumni say they are willing to be a mentor. This is an amazing and stable statistic as seen across hundreds of our clients' digital career communities.

On the other hand, we have seen the number of people who formally enter mentoring relationship to be, relative to this 70% number, significantly lower.

So, how can one explain this difference?

One possible answer is that, although alumni are willing to mentor others, they themselves do not have a need for alumni mentoring. Possibly, but this goes against lots of research that I have written about previously.

An alternative and more likely answer is that our definition of what a mentoring relationship means needs updating.

For some mentoring relationships, be it alumni-alumni mentoring or alumni-student mentoring, are an intense, formal relationship that is 'entered into' almost like marriage.

The reality is that most alumni mentoring relationships are not like that and do not need to be structured like that. The 'marriage' model of mentoring, offered by alumni career services, may only be suitable for a minority of alumni and students looking for much more long-term advice and support.

I believe most mentoring relationships have a diverse range of intensity and formality.

Let me use the case study of the Smith School of Business in Canada.

What is striking about the success that the Smith School of Business has had building this mentoring network is the variety of alumni and student networking experiences they have facilitated.

Yes, they have enabled full 'marriage' type mentoring, but they have also facilitated more informal 'flash' mentoring such as being 'available for a coffee', 'willing to make advice' or offering to 'make introductions to my connections'.

In fact, if you look at the number of unique networking conversations then approximately 50% of the network has been involved in some form of alumni networking or mentoring.

When it comes to mentoring, we need to still believe in marriage, but perhaps we need to recognize other types of relationships too.

Digital career communities need to be less well defined and more open to what alumni and students really want.

We may need to re-think how we offer our alumni career services going forward.

Should Alumni Mentoring Be A Dating App or An Arranged Marriage?

I see a clear and positive trend of schools strengthening the career services they offer their alumni.

This is shown by a visible effort being made by schools to improve the collaboration between their alumni relations and career services departments. In fact, many schools now have a specific team devoted to alumni career services. This make senses as it is an area where schools can show a tangible value proposition to their alumni.

At the heart of this trend is mentoring - both alumni mentoring and student mentoring. In short, everyone is talking about mentoring.

Yet, what is the best way to facilitate alumni mentoring program?

Should a mentoring program be run on the traditional but resource-heavy approach of the school being the 'middle-man' and manually pairing off mentors and mentees? Or, is this the place where technology should take the lead and automate the mentoring matching process?

At the 2015 Graduway Leaders Summit held at Oxford University, an esteemed panel were asked this very question.

I think two key points emerged from the discussion. Firstly, which type of alumni mentoring relationships are most likely to succeed?

Eva Kubu, Director of Career Services at Princeton University, highlighted the need to drastically change the way we match (whether manually or on-line.) In her view, the focus needs to be about facilitating connections between alumni based upon shared interests, shared affiliations and shared intent on the purpose of connecting. In her words...

"Most of the typical ways that matching occurs does not get to the core of what drives connections - namely shared interests and passions."

The route to obtaining meaningful and authentic relationships is understanding the true passions of your alumni.

The second area of discussion dealt with how best to facilitate alumni mentoring, 'high touch' or 'high tech'.

Julia Sanchez, Head of Global Alumni Relations at IE Business School, cautioned a more balanced approach. On the one hand, a 'high-tech' approach clearly has a contribution to make in the facilitation of alumni networks especially when your alumni diaspora is spread across the world. Julia highlighted the geo-location technology IE use in their app to help alumni find other alumni physically near to them.

She however also cautioned that technology alone would not solve all the mentoring needs and cited specific examples of where her team had made important contributions to facilitating individual connections.

Where do you think the balance on facilitating mentoring should be, high touch or high tech? What is the right balance?

Is there a role for schools in the matching process of mentors? How critical is mentoring in building a career community?

I would welcome your thoughts.

The Tech Revolution in Alumni Networks

I had the privilege of speaking on a panel discussion at the ASU-GSV Summit in San Diego, discussing the latest trends in student and alumni career services.

The panel was entitled 'The Tech Revolution in College Career Networks'. Featured alongside me were the following distinguished colleagues Andy Chan, Leah Lommel, Preston Silverman, Farouk Dey and Gordon Jones.

The discussion covered areas such as why we are seeing today the focus on career services (both student and alumni careers) and its supporting technology including the rising cost of college, the changing employment landscape and the need for scalable career service solutions (including alumni student mentoring). It also covered what these leading institutions are doing to embrace this revolution and advice to vendors on what they need to be doing better as well.

My own biggest learning from the discussion was to hear career services professionals in Higher Education talk about the shift of purpose in their own roles, as Stanford's Farouk Dey put it,

"From being transaction providers of career placement, to providers of career education."

Providers of career education should not focus on placing students into jobs but rather equipping and educating students on how to develop their professional community of mentors, door openers and support network which appears to be the main path to their career goals.

This got me thinking that probably the biggest obstacle to this technology revolution in college alumni networks has probably nothing to do with technology. Rather, I see the biggest obstacle being a cultural one. Colleges need to understand that to successfully deliver on this new career services vision and leveraging technology requires the end of the silo thinking around the management of students' careers. The silo that I see daily between career services and alumni relations that must be torn down.

Technology has a huge role to play in supporting the revolution.

Yet I have left with the open question. Is the Higher Education world ready and capable of embracing the cultural changes, in particular, the cross departmental collaboration, required to unleash this revolution?

I would welcome your thoughts.

The Anatomy of the Ideal Mentoring Program

The success of a mentoring program relies largely on the state of the relationship between the Career Services and the Alumni Relations departments and whether they choose to coordinate and collaborate.

Once they have chosen to collaborate, the question is who should take the lead? Should Career Services lead because the goal is to progress the students career? Or, should Alumni Relations take things forward because their role is to engage alumni?

Historically, there are Career Service offices that have existed on college campuses and then there are Alumni Offices in separate buildings, each with separate budgets and different staff. For years, these two offices have been different entities and have often struggled to fully align their priorities.

In the last two decades, members of staff from either Alumni Relations or Careers have effectively said "let's involve alumni more strategically by making them mentors to boost our students' career options." Unlocking this potential hinged largely on the collaboration between the Alumni and Career offices.

As a whole, this strategy has been beneficial for both mentoring programs and reducing tension between Alumni and Career offices. However, effective collaboration has not happened across the board.

Today, there are still plenty of Alumni Office teams - especially at large, public, highly decentralized universities in the United States - who sit miles away from their colleagues in the Careers Offices and have practically no relationship with them. Some even have an adversarial relationship with their central Career Services office.

There remains huge potential for these two critical offices to work much closer together. The future of successful mentoring programs require collaboration to be the norm and not the exception. Change is happening.

CHAPTER THREE

Mentoring Best Practices

How to Yield 42% Participation in an Alumni Mentoring Program?

Mentoring is clearly a buzz word now in the world of alumni relations and career services.

Indeed, most education institutions would like to have a successful alumnus mentoring or student mentoring program but may be confused as how best to make this happen.

At the Graduway Leaders Summit at UCLA, I had the privilege of hearing a joint presentation by Katie Davy, Executive Director, Alumni Career Programs and Partnerships at UCLA and Michael Schurder, Vice President Product at Graduway on how to build a successful mentoring program.

UCLA have used Graduway's on-line alumni directory / alumni software to power their alumni network.

I wanted to add three personal thoughts of my own on helping schools build a successful mentoring program but with the emphasis on three 'mistakes' I believe schools need to avoid.

Firstly, I believe some schools become metric obsessed and lose sight of the goal. They would like to track and follow every possible click or interaction (many of which are not relevant)

while forgetting to focus on the only metric that really counts - how many mentoring relationships are being formed.

Secondly, some schools tend to become micro managers. They want to co-ordinate and control every aspect of the mentor-mentee relationship. I believe the balance can get out of hand and stifle the natural interactions in a mentoring relationship. Your mentors are experienced professionals and do not want to be micro-managed. Schools need to facilitate these relationships and not micro-manage them.

Thirdly, I believe some schools focus their efforts disproportionately on the mentee (students) and neglect the mentor (alumni). Schools make the classic mistake of building a stand-alone mentoring platform or alumni software without any thought on what will motivate the mentor to actively and regularly visit that platform. A successful mentoring program needs to be built as part of a wider alumni/mentor network.

The result of these mistakes is that you can end up with a program that tracks every possible interaction, controls every aspect of the relationship and supports the mentee every step of the way and yet still fails.

Avoid these simple mistakes and I believe you will be much closer to achieving the type of strong results UCLA achieved.

Have you built a successful mentoring program? Can you provide feedback on mistakes you made which others can learn from?

Finally, which is the most important factor in your view for a mentoring program to succeed?

I would welcome your thoughts.

ONE TWO

SIX SEVE

ELEVEN T

SIXTEEN S

TWENTY-

The Value of Engaging Your Young Alumni

Class reunions are traditional and commonplace. They are also effective.

They enable alumni to catch up and re-connect with their alma mater. They also provide an additional - and powerful - benefit. They give people the opportunity to network and advance their careers.

What better way to demonstrate the value of mentoring to alumni?

If alumni are to become your institution's mentors, they should not only be engaged and emotionally connected, they should also see the added value that mentoring can bring to their own careers.

Why Target Young Alumni?

Young alumni are engaged with their alma mater and are often passionate about recruiting more students. So, use this energy! Young alumni should be seen as Admissions Ambassadors, helping to help recruit high school students to come to your University or institution.

What we find when we look at institutions that do this kind of admissions activity is not surprising. Their alumni volunteer rates are very high, the likelihood that these alumni will attend events is also very high, as is the chance of them becoming donors - three very important wins.

Careers Offices should also engage young alumni. They understand the type of person who comes out of your institution, and they are proud to be connected to their alma mater, so they should be encouraged to recruit your current graduating class.

Whether it's recruiting younger students to your institution or professionally recruiting your graduating students, make sure to engage your young alumni!

This essay was based upon an interview with Chris Marshall.

Chris Marshall is a senior higher education advancement professional with 17 years of alumni engagement experience at Lehigh University and Cornell University.

In addition, Chris has five years' experience as an alumni engagement consultant for over 100 clients at one of the top alumni engagement and philanthropic consulting practices in the United States - Grenzebach Glier and Associates (GG+A).

Chris currently serves as the President of Graduway, North America and is recognized as a top thought leader in Alumni Relations.

What is Stopping You from Fulfilling Your Potential?

In the ideal world, where Alumni Relations and Career Services fully collaborate, there are still other barriers that can stifle the functioning of a successful mentoring program...

1. Cultivate 'the love'

A study, conducted by Alumni Monitor in 2015, polled more than 1,100 alumni of U.S. higher education institutions. It looked at the correlation between fundraising efforts at schools and alumni sentiments. The results confirmed what we would have suspected - that the emotional connection needs to take priority; we need to engage first and ask second.

If you do not first cultivate "the love" for the alma mater, chances of success with your mentoring program are slim. You can have all the resources there for your mentors, but this will go untapped if there is no desire to engage.

Institutions need to get students and alumni thinking that they are part of a continuum – that older and younger graduates and students are all connected. The expectation should be that if you need help, you can get it, and if you can give it, you do.

2. Budget

As with any program implementation, monetary concerns are at the heart of the discussion. While technology can be costly, it can also save a lot of time and resources.

The true question is how much is your institution willing to invest in their alumni, and how much of an investment does the institution believe they are worth?

The simple calculation is:
Value – Price = Cost.

3. Resources

Your institution may not always have the available resources to implement a mentoring program. There are several factors to consider such as: the amount of staff, the percentage of graduating students and the full-time employees in the career services or Alumni office. A program like this requires a team who are willing to work towards the institutional goals and these staff may not exist on the campus. There are many resources available online outlining best practices for mentoring which are easy to follow.

4. Time / Planning

The issue of timing and planning a mentoring program is a double-edged sword as a barrier to the success of a mentoring program. If an institution decides to micro-manage each facet of a mentoring relationship, this can hinder the scalability of the program and is not best practice. That said, if an institution invested the planning stage of their mentoring program with technology, the facilitation and the manual period it would have taken is reduced.

I hope this article helps to clarify and prepare you for the biggest challenges you will need to over-come to optimize your mentoring program.

Sheila Curran, CEO of Curran Consulting Group.

In 2008, Sheila left academia to start an organizational strategy consulting business. The Curran Consulting Group is a boutique strategy and organizational firm that focuses on higher education consulting.

Recognized as a subject matter expert in the careers field, her work is informed by 12 years of experience directing career services at Brown University and Duke University as well as 13 years serving in high level positions in human resources.

Say Goodbye to Your Graduating Class. Forever.

The countdown has started.

It is already March and, for many schools, it is just 12 weeks until graduation.

Time to celebrate? Well, not if you are involved in the career services or alumni relations department of an education institution.

Let me be a little provocative. For what percentage of your students will graduation be the last time you ever hear from them again? 30%? 40%? Or worse?

For many of your graduating students, the commencement ceremony will be the beginning of a lifetime of zero interaction with your institution.

The big question is why. Why do schools lose touch so quickly?

The technical answer is that the first summer post-graduation will, for many of your alumni, mark big changes in their personal and professional lives.

They will probably start a new role or job. They will probably move location. And, of course, they will probably have new contact information. Within weeks, all the contact information you hold on these individuals (address, email, phone number) will be out of date.

This still leaves the underlying question – why. Why do schools lose contact so quickly even if these changes are happening?

The answer is because many schools often only decide to stay in touch with their alumni after they have already left.

In short, schools leave it too late.

In an ideal world, your institution will start to build its culture of philanthropy and alumni engagement not on the last day but the first day of school.

For those interested in a strategic approach to this, please see Elise Betz, Executive Director of Alumni Relations from the University of Pennsylvania, who gave an inspiring keynote speech at the Graduway Leaders Summit. Her talk, *"Cultivating Roots: Building a Culture of Student Philanthropy and Engagement"*, was a bold example of how a school (albeit a top one) can strategically invest in their culture of giving with an eye on the very long term.

However, what if your school is unable to think that long term and needs a solution in place within the next few weeks?

Here are three tips for you:

1. Connect via social networks

Get connected with your graduating students via their social networks. Alumni may well change jobs and location, but their Facebook and LinkedIn connection details will stay constant.

2. Make them part of your digital career community

While it is understandable that you only want to reward students with membership of the alumni body once they graduate, it is simply too late. Facilitating alumni networking and mentoring is critical. Invite your students to join your digital career community and benefit from finding a mentor. Alumni networks are for students as well!

3. Give them a reason to stay connected

Show them before they graduate how being part of an exclusive alumni network can help them both professionally and socially and provide access to life-long mentoring.

The clock is ticking. You still have time to save your connection with your Graduating Class, but you need to get moving now.

Alumni networking and mentoring seems to be a big part of the answer.

I would welcome your thoughts.

Are You Crazy? Don't Build It Yourself. Buy.

So, I asked the VP Alumni Relations 'why did your institution build its new IT system rather than buy it from an external vendor?'

And, the answer went something like this...

You are right. It was a mistake. Our IT department is made up of very talented people. We decided to build it ourselves, but it is not a scratch on what you are showing me. In fact, I feel sick seeing what you are showing me, knowing that our product will never look as good, and we have invested so much time and money.

I can provide some very practical arguments about why it almost never pays for an education institution to build rather than buy their own new alumni software, on-line alumni directory, website, database, mentoring software, alumni networking platform or communication tool.

1. Cost

It will cost more.

2. Time

It will take longer.

3. Quality

It will likely be less good, particularly from the user experience.

Even if one were to make allowances for the fact that your institution has truly unique requirements and customizations, I still do not believe that it would make sense to build your own alumni software.

I have also noticed a strange phenomenon. The larger and wealthier the institution is, the more likely it is to build its own mentoring or alumni software and, to be blunt, the more clunky and outdated its systems look. Wealth in this case seems like a distinct disadvantage.

I have sat with some of the world's best universities in rooms filled with their talented IT people who could build almost anything. Here lies the root of the problem. Schools build because they can, not because they should.

The discussion over whether a school should build or buy is overtaken by the simple fact that they have enough internal talent to build. However, this is not a sufficient reason to do so.

Let me use the crude example of a car. Would you build or buy your own car? For most of us, this is a simple decision as we are unable to build, so the only option is to buy. However, imagine if you were a very talented engineer, would you really build your own car in your garage or buy one from an experienced automobile company?

Just because you can is not a sufficient reason to build.

Rather, the discussion should be centred around strategic focus. What does your organization do better than anyone else in the world? What is your unique expertise? Where should you be investing your personnel and conversely? Where should you be utilizing external experts?

In our fast-moving world, I think the discussion is at long last moving decisively in favor of buying because of the emergence of one new factor, namely access to innovation.

I was speaking to a vice-chancellor at a very prestigious institution. They have very talented IT personnel and budget is simply not an issue. In the past, this organization had always built everything internally. Not anymore. This institution has decided to buy its new database from an established industry provider. Their motivation was simple - it is all about innovation. Using a database from Blackbaud or Salesforce meant them having access to an ecosystem of partner vendors providing literally hundreds of innovative products each year.

This was the clear tipping point. Even the biggest university can no longer innovate in this specialized field at the rate of dedicated vendors. If cost, time or quality arguments do not work, then perhaps the final knock-out punch is about having continuous access to cutting edge innovation.

The days of schools building their own systems and alumni software seem to be over.

Has your organization recently entered a build versus buy discussion?

What was the deciding factor for you?

What would you recommend as the best way to facilitate such a sensitive internal discussion?

I would welcome your thoughts.

The Benefits of Flash Mentoring

Today, **mentoring is often like speed dating.** A mentor can commit to having a ten minute conversation with a student interested in his/her career.

All it takes is a connection, through a digital platform or email, and a meeting is booked. In those ten minutes, the alum answers whatever questions the student has and then he or she is done – that's it.

After that conversation, there's no "I'll see you for coffee next week" or "when's our next appointment?" It can literally be one interaction and finished!

More alumni want to engage in this type of mentoring because it is flexible, and it gives them and the student an instant return without a long-term commitment.

Thought Leaders call this new phenomenon 'flash mentoring', 'speed mentoring' and 'micro volunteering'.

In other words, there is a clear sunrise and a clear sunset. The mentor isn't doing this for the next two years, they're only doing it for those ten minutes. It's a chance for the mentor to have more interactions with more students and help them with their career paths.

As a result, I believe we need to drastically change the way we match mentors and the way we think about valuable engagement. The focus needs to be about facilitating connections between alumni, based upon shared interests, affiliations and intent.

Most of the traditional ways of matching do not get to the core of what drives connections - namely shared interests and passions.

Finding and facilitating a common passion between alumni and students is difficult, and it is not something that can be done instantly. Like all relationships, this must be done organically.

Speed mentoring is valuable and so are deeper mentoring relationships. For both, the key to matching is understanding - and where possible documenting - the true interests, affiliations and intent of both your alumni and your students.

7 Top Tips to Improve Your Mentoring

1 Embrace the digital tools out there to help pair mentors and mentees.

2 Keep that human touch where possible.

3 Facilitate contact between mentors and mentees, but don't become overbearing.

4 Give options: there is no right or wrong way to be a mentor or mentee!

5 Don't limit mentoring to just one group: just because it's been 30 years since you graduated does not mean you don't need a mentor!

6 Collaboration between Alumni and Career Services is the key to success.

7 Share success stories about mentoring relationships that have made a difference.

Connect
With Graduway

I would be delighted to hear your thoughts on the articles in this special report.

You can reach me at **daniel.cohen@graduway.com.**

I look forward to hearing from you,

Daniel Cohen
Founder and CEO of Graduway

Empowering
Alumni Relations

24349510R00031

Made in the USA
Columbia, SC
22 August 2018